This Bucket List Journal Belongs To:

_____

The World is yours to explore

My Bucket List

My Bucket List

My Bucket List

My Bucket List

Bucket List

What

Why

How

Completed

Date

Where

With

Notes/Thoughts/Memories

Would I Do It Again?   yes ☐   no ☐

Journal

Bucket List

What

Why

How

Completed

Date

Where

With

Notes/Thoughts/Memories

Would I Do It Again?   yes ☐   no ☐

Journal

Bucket List

What

Why

How

Completed

Date

Where

With

Notes/Thoughts/Memories

Would I Do It Again?   yes ☐   no ☐

Journal

Bucket List

What

Why

How

Completed

Date

Where

With

Notes/Thoughts/Memories

Would I Do It Again? ☐ yes ☐ no

Journal

Bucket List

What

Why

How

Completed

Date

Where

With

Notes/Thoughts/Memories

Would I Do It Again? yes ☐   no ☐

Journal

Bucket List

What

Why How

Completed

Date Where

With

Notes/Thoughts/Memories

Would I Do It Again? yes no

Journal

Bucket List

What

Why

How

Completed

Date

Where

With

Notes/Thoughts/Memories

Would I Do It Again? yes ☐ no ☐

Journal

Bucket List

What

Why　　　　　　　　　　**How**

Completed

Date　　　　　　　　　　**Where**

With

Notes/Thoughts/Memories

Would I Do It Again?　　☐ yes　　☐ no

Journal

Bucket List

What

Why

How

Completed

Date

Where

With

Notes/Thoughts/Memories

Would I Do It Again?   yes ☐   no ☐

Journal

Bucket List

What

Why

How

Completed

Date

Where

With

Notes/Thoughts/Memories

Would I Do It Again?   yes ☐   no ☐

Journal

Bucket List

What

Why

How

Completed

Date

Where

With

Notes/Thoughts/Memories

Would I Do It Again?　　yes ☐　　no ☐

Journal

Bucket List

What

Why

How

Completed

Date

Where

With

Notes/Thoughts/Memories

Would I Do It Again? ☐ yes ☐ no

Journal

Bucket List

What

Why

How

Completed

Date

Where

With

Notes/Thoughts/Memories

Would I Do It Again? yes ☐ no ☐

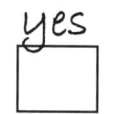

Journal

Bucket List

What

Why

How

Completed

Date

Where

With

Notes/Thoughts/Memories

Would I Do It Again?   yes ☐   no ☐

Journal

Bucket List

What

Why

How

Completed

Date

Where

With

Notes/Thoughts/Memories

Would I Do It Again? yes ☐ no ☐

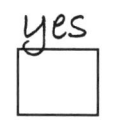

Journal

Bucket List

What

Why

How

Completed

Date

Where

With

Notes/Thoughts/Memories

Would I Do It Again? ☐ yes ☐ no

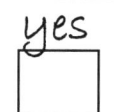

Journal

Bucket List

What

Why

How

Completed

Date

Where

With

Notes/Thoughts/Memories

Would I Do It Again? yes ☐ no ☐

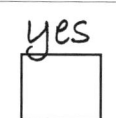

Journal

Bucket List

What

Why   **How**

Completed

Date   **Where**

With

Notes/Thoughts/Memories

Would I Do It Again?   yes ☐   no ☐

Journal

Bucket List

What

Why

How

Completed

Date

Where

With

Notes/Thoughts/Memories

Would I Do It Again?   yes ☐   no ☐

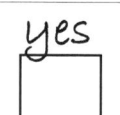

Journal

Bucket List

What

Why

How

Completed

Date

Where

With

Notes/Thoughts/Memories

Would I Do It Again?   yes ☐   no ☐

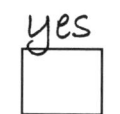

Journal

Bucket List

What

Why

How

Completed

Date

Where

With

Notes/Thoughts/Memories

Would I Do It Again? yes ☐ no ☐

Journal

Bucket List

What

Why

How

Completed

Date

Where

With

Notes/Thoughts/Memories

Would I Do It Again? yes ☐ no ☐

Journal

Bucket List

What

Why

How

Completed

Date

Where

With

Notes/Thoughts/Memories

Would I Do It Again? yes ☐ no ☐

Journal

Bucket List

What

Why

How

Completed

Date

Where

With

Notes/Thoughts/Memories

Would I Do It Again?   yes ☐   no ☐

Journal

Bucket List

What

Why

How

Completed

Date

Where

With

Notes/Thoughts/Memories

Would I Do It Again?   yes ☐   no ☐

Journal

Bucket List

What

Why

How

Completed

Date

Where

With

Notes/Thoughts/Memories

Would I Do It Again? yes ☐ no ☐

Journal

Bucket List

What

Why **How**

Completed

Date **Where**

With

Notes/Thoughts/Memories

Would I Do It Again? ☐ yes ☐ no

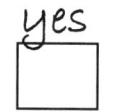

Journal

Bucket List

What

Why

How

Completed

Date

Where

With

Notes/Thoughts/Memories

Would I Do It Again? yes ☐ no ☐

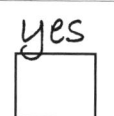

Journal

Bucket List

What

Why

How

Completed

Date

Where

With

Notes/Thoughts/Memories

Would I Do It Again?   yes ☐   no ☐

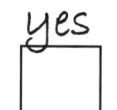

Journal

Bucket List

What

Why

How

Completed

Date

Where

With

Notes/Thoughts/Memories

Would I Do It Again? ☐ yes ☐ no

Journal

Bucket List

What

Why

How

Completed

Date

Where

With

Notes/Thoughts/Memories

Would I Do It Again? yes ☐ no ☐

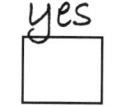

Journal

Bucket List

What

Why

How

Completed

Date

Where

With

Notes/Thoughts/Memories

Would I Do It Again?   yes ☐   no ☐

Journal

Bucket List

What

Why

How

Completed

Date   Where

With

Notes/Thoughts/Memories

Would I Do It Again?   yes ☐   no ☐

Journal

Bucket List

What

Why

How

Completed

Date

Where

With

Notes/Thoughts/Memories

Would I Do It Again? yes ☐ no ☐

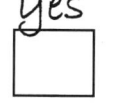

Journal

Bucket List

What

Why

How

Completed

Date

Where

With

Notes/Thoughts/Memories

Would I Do It Again? yes ☐ no ☐

Journal

Bucket List

What

Why

How

Completed

Date

Where

With

Notes/Thoughts/Memories

Would I Do It Again?   yes ☐   no ☐

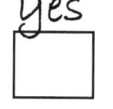

Journal

Bucket List

What

Why

How

Completed

Date

Where

With

Notes/Thoughts/Memories

Would I Do It Again?   yes ☐   no ☐

Journal

Bucket List

What

Why

How

Completed

Date

Where

With

Notes/Thoughts/Memories

Would I Do It Again?   yes ☐   no ☐

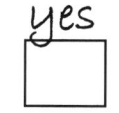

Journal

Bucket List

What

Why

How

Completed

Date

Where

With

Notes/Thoughts/Memories

Would I Do It Again? yes ☐ no ☐

Journal

Bucket List

What

Why

How

Completed

Date

Where

With

Notes/Thoughts/Memories

Would I Do It Again? yes ☐ no ☐

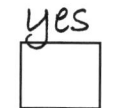

Journal

Bucket List

What

Why

How

Completed

Date

Where

With

Notes/Thoughts/Memories

Would I Do It Again? yes ☐ no ☐

Journal

Bucket List

What

Why

How

Completed

Date

Where

With

Notes/Thoughts/Memories

Would I Do It Again? yes ☐   no ☐

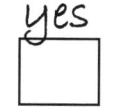

Journal

Bucket List

What

Why

How

Completed

Date

Where

With

Notes/Thoughts/Memories

Would I Do It Again?   yes ☐   no ☐

Journal

Bucket List

What

Why

How

Completed

Date

Where

With

Notes/Thoughts/Memories

Would I Do It Again? yes ☐ no ☐

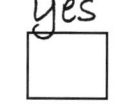

Journal

Bucket List

What

Why

How

Completed

Date

Where

With

Notes/Thoughts/Memories

Would I Do It Again?   yes ☐   no ☐

Journal

Bucket List

What

Why

How

Completed

Date

Where

With

Notes/Thoughts/Memories

Would I Do It Again? yes ☐ no ☐

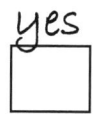

Journal

Bucket List

What

Why

How

Completed

Date

Where

With

Notes/Thoughts/Memories

Would I Do It Again? yes ☐ no ☐

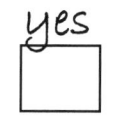

Journal

Bucket List

What

Why

How

Completed

Date

Where

With

Notes/Thoughts/Memories

Would I Do It Again?   yes ☐   no ☐

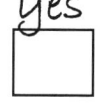

Journal

Bucket List

What

Why

How

Completed

Date

Where

With

Notes/Thoughts/Memories

Would I Do It Again?   yes ☐   no ☐

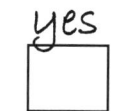

Journal

Bucket List

What

Why

How

Completed

Date

Where

With

Notes/Thoughts/Memories

Would I Do It Again? yes ☐ no ☐

Journal

Bucket List

What

Why

How

Completed

Date

Where

With

Notes/Thoughts/Memories

Would I Do It Again?   yes ☐   no ☐

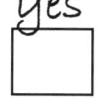

Journal

Bucket List

What

Why

How

Completed

Date

Where

With

Notes/Thoughts/Memories

Would I Do It Again?   yes ☐   no ☐

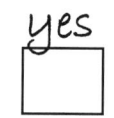

Journal

Bucket List

What

Why

How

Completed

Date

Where

With

Notes/Thoughts/Memories

Would I Do It Again?   yes ☐   no ☐

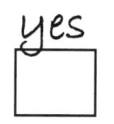

Journal

Bucket List

What

Why

How

Completed

Date

Where

With

Notes/Thoughts/Memories

Would I Do It Again? yes ☐ no ☐

Journal

Bucket List

What

Why

How

Completed

Date

Where

With

Notes/Thoughts/Memories

Would I Do It Again? yes ☐ no ☐

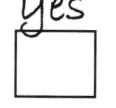

Journal

Bucket List

What

Why

How

Completed

Date

Where

With

Notes/Thoughts/Memories

Would I Do It Again?   yes ☐   no ☐

Journal

Bucket List

What

Why

How

Completed

Date

Where

With

Notes/Thoughts/Memories

Would I Do It Again?   yes ☐   no ☐

Journal

Bucket List

What

Why

How

Completed

Date

Where

With

Notes/Thoughts/Memories

Would I Do It Again?   yes ☐   no ☐

Journal

Bucket List

What

Why

How

Completed

Date

Where

With

Notes/Thoughts/Memories

Would I Do It Again?   yes ☐   no ☐

Journal

Bucket List

What

Why

How

Completed

Date

Where

With

Notes/Thoughts/Memories

Would I Do It Again? yes ☐ no ☐

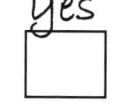

Journal

Made in the USA
Middletown, DE
08 March 2022